HE LOVES ME NOT

Buried Tears of Betrayed Love

Kimesha Coleman

This book is dedicated with love to my mother,

in loving memory of my aunt,
Lorene Houston,
a lady filled with "genuine love",

and to the many survivors of abuse.

Copyright © 2015 Kimesha Coleman

All rights reserved. No part of this book may be used or reproduced in any manner whatsoever without the written permission of the Publisher. Printed in the United States of America. For more information address Kimesha Coleman, PO Box 1109, Cedar Hill, TX 75106.

Names and identifying characteristics of people in the book have been changed to protect the privacy of the individuals.

Unless otherwise indicated, all Scriptures quotations are taken from the Holy Bible, New Living Translation, copyright © 1996, 2004. Used by permission of Tyndale House Publishers, Inc., Carol Stream, Illinois 60188, All rights reserved.

Scriptures quoted from The Holy Bible, New Century Version, copyright © 1987, 1988, 1991, by Word Publishing, Dallas, Texas 75039, Used by permission.

ISBN: 978-0-692-40806-3

Table of Contents

Introduction 1

Chapter One

    Unconditional Love 5

Chapter Two

    My First Love 13

Chapter Three

    Same Man Different Name 33

Chapter Four

    Healing 47

Chapter Five

    Self-Esteem 71

Chapter Six

    Victim to Victor 81

20 Principles of Loving Yourself More 91

Victims' Bill of Rights 93

About the Author 95

References 97

Introduction

Like myself, you too may have asked what is love?

> **Love is** patient, love is kind. It does not envy, it does not boast, it is not proud. It does not dishonor others, it is not self-seeking, it is not easily angered, it keeps no record of wrongs. Love does not delight in evil but rejoices with the truth. It always protects, always trusts, always hopes, always perseveres.
> —1 Corinthians 13:4-7, *NLT*

In the Bible, Paul describes love using the above details giving a clear description of the **actions** surrounding *LOVE*. Merriam Webster's dictionary describes love as (noun) "a warm affection based on admiration, benevolence, or common interest, and as a (verb) to hold dear, cherish."

We all have a different view of what love is and different love languages. For some you may like affection or being touched often. Some may like to be showered with gifts in order to feel loved. Others, may require lots of quality time spent with loved ones and friends. However some may like to hear the words "I love you" often or other words of affirmation in order to feel cared for. Lastly, some prefer acts of service, where someone uses their skills

Introduction

and abilities to display their love. You may have two of the love languages described above, but one may be more prominent than the other.

Growing up as a child, my view of love was simplified down to a hug or a gift. The gifts and affection were my primary feelings of love. A feeling of uncertainty filled my spirit after the very same people that had showed me acceptance and love were now giving me a great deal of pain by their crossed actions of untrustworthiness.

We are taught to love unconditionally and without limits. Unconditional love does not mean you allow someone to harm or abuse you and still keep them in a close proximity.

As my heart became filled with vengeance and anger, I wanted someone to pay for my pain- pay for my emotional poisoning. It was like a thorn in my thumb that wouldn't go away. I know it is there but yet incapable to act in a way to relieve myself. The pain flooded my life with self-destructive behavior as I tried to cover up the hurt. I put on my mask everyday as most of us do to cover up the tears buried beneath the pain of betrayed love.

Looking back I realized the cycle of betrayal had taken root when the agreement of unconditional love was broken as a child. I was so detached from the world, lacked affection, and deserted intimacy in its tracks. But yet looked desperately for love, only to find another wolf in sheep clothing waiting to fill my heart with tears of regret.

He Loves Me Not

This book was written to help readers gain clarity of what love is NOT, give you a view of the pattern of abuse, give practical steps on how to heal from abuse, and discover the greatest love of all. You.

CHAPTER ONE

Unconditional Love

We all long to be loved. Love or the feeling of affection and admiration is first established by our immediate family. The essence of a family- a connection at the core of birthday parties, holidays, and backyard barbeques- places a sense of belonging and creates a bond of unity. A group of people sharing the same goals and values while being committed to one another just as passionately. Family is an everlasting relationship and so is the love that is given within it. To be betrayed by your family can take the air out of your lungs and leave you gasping for breath. It leaves you with endless unanswered questions, anger, and resentment following you from childhood, way into your adult life, and sometimes until death. Some may even say this is the ultimate betrayal of life.

First Betrayal
Tim was adored by everyone. I was always glad to see him,

especially since he brought gifts when he came to visit. I remember the tootsie roll can filled with candy he would bring for me. After eating all the candy I would use the can to put money in it.

My mother had married his brother, Fred. They had a very large family and would come over on Friday evenings. The living room would be filled with smoke from cigarettes, music from Donna Summers playing in the background, a good game of Spades alongside with a keg of beer. Did you say party? No need to go to the club, as we had our own every Friday night. I would watch as some of them would become too intoxicated and couldn't make it back home on account of all the beer that was guzzled down. I typically found them throwing up and passing out in the living room.

We had a two bedroom, one bath home in Oak Cliff, Texas where my younger sister, mom, stepdad, and I lived. One night while asleep in my bed, I was awakened by a voice. This voice was a familiar one, but yet the tone seemed dark and evil as he leaned over me. He was looking for a trade. I knew it was wrong and denied him of what he wanted, holding on tight to the covers on my bed.

In my mind I thought "how could he just come in here while my parents were sleeping in the next room?" Didn't they know? I looked over at the bedroom door; I wanted my stepdad to come in and rescue me, but he never came. I didn't quite understand why no one noticed him slipping into my room.

I'm not really sure how many late-night visits occurred, but they continued for a while. The money and gifts stop coming, as this person was no longer my favorite uncle. The happiness and excitement I once had in life disappeared.

I began to sleep with all my clothes. Sometimes playing sleep hoping he would leave, closing my eyes so tight that I would fall into a deep sleep, even blackout. When morning came I would find my pants pulled half way down my legs.

There was a particular night I remember him telling me, "If you don't let me do it now, it's gonna hurt later." I really didn't know what he would do to me. I would blackout, but those words made my body tighten from the thought of him going between my legs. I didn't like what he was doing to me. I was frightened and confused. I felt hopeless and wondered why no one seemed to care or even ask me about what was going on. He left outside the room only to come back with the Vaseline jar.

He instructed me with these firm words, "Don't tell your mother, she'll be mad at you." It was as if he was a friend confiding a deep secret to me and saying, "Don't tell anyone, they won't believe you anyway if you did." My mind raced and now I was even more confused. He was hurting me. I wanted to tell someone. I wanted it to stop.

The Secret

From the age of 7 to 10 years old, Tim (my uncle) repeatedly came into my room when he would take advantage of me. On the last occasion, he leaned in to kiss me on my mouth, only centimeters from my face. Not sure what come over me. I pulled my arm back and slapped him with all my might in the face. Tim never came back to my room.

A few years had gone by before I finally blurted out to my mom and stepdad what Tim had been doing to me at night while everyone was asleep. Unfortunately, Tim was right. After making the big announcement, the response to the abuse was even more devastating than the actual abuse itself had been. No one responded to anything I had just told them. No questions, no remorse, no sympathy, just silence. It was if I was in a real life Twilight Zone. The help and resources were right in front of me, but no one heard my cry.

Child molestation is a common generational secret that few talk about or even address. This well kept secret destroys so many children and the lives of adults. It is reported that there exists a link to drug and substance abuse, prostitution, depression, and most suicides. Fact is, these symptoms do not only found and affect the victim of abuse, but also the offender (the abuser) and the denier (the person or people that know about these inappropriate behaviors and act as if it's not happening).

Signs of Abuse

A child molester can be a parent, grandparent, sibling, stepparent, other family members, teacher, coach or clergyman. They all follow a pattern with the goal of emotionally and mentally seducing a child into trusting them. They call this grooming. You must understand how the process works in order to identify the signs when it's happening. Molesters focus on empowering the child with a "bad secret" that is used to manipulate and control them.

A child victim of molestation may show signs of the following:

- Isolation
- Masturbating
- Bedwetting or acting like a younger child (regression)
- Sexual acting out behaviors towards other children
- Protective withdrawal – distancing themselves
- Thumb sucking
- Uncontrollable crying
- Aggressive acting out
- Poor self concept
- Suicide attempts
- Sexual drawings

Child molestation can happen at home, work, school, church, or a day care facility. The action of molestation may include asking or pressuring a child to engage in sexual activities. Victims usually have more than one offender. I mentioned only one abuser during this period of my life in this book. I was also fondled by a second uncle and female cousin on one or more occasions.

My once healthy view of love and family was distorted through the betrayal of trust by a loved one. For 27 years, I was emotionally dysfunctional, still held captive to a mind of the frightened child waiting to be rescued, waiting to be heard, and reassured that no one would hurt me. I was in a grown person's body carrying the emotional functions of an 11 year old child.

As a child I never received the support or love I desperately needed to get through this trauma. I wanted that long hug to make me feel safe. I wanted that soft kiss on the forehead that said "I love you." I wanted to know that I mattered through that one simple question I never heard; "Are you okay?" I wanted to have that hard conversation to get things out in the open and to know it wasn't my fault. I needed to hear I wasn't a bad person. I wanted empathy and to know everything would be alright.

As I interviewed women survivors of domestic abuse, I wasn't surprised to hear they too had been molested as a child. In many cases, they too had been abused by a family member and were left suffering from the shame and guilt while the abuser walked around freely.

NOTES

Unconditional Love

CHAPTER TWO

My First Love

Do you remember your first crush? The goose bumps, stomach butterflies, and twinkle in your eyes along with adrenaline running through your body? You could hardly wait to get to school, church, or to the playground just get a look at him. Looking at him gave you a natural high, a tingling in your toes and a sense of yearning and desire. Was this love? You dreamed about your first kiss, and how happy you'd be walking along side by side with him holding his hand.

Dating, what a fun and exciting part of growing up. However too often, parents fail to communicate about dating to their teens or discuss what a healthy relationship consists of. Girls especially are raised to be submissive and have a mixed message about who they are supposed to be. If they were exposed to abuse at home this adds even more confusion. The lack of education on abuse may lead a teen to believe this is a normal and acceptable behavior.

The Relationship

It was Saturday night. My mother and her sisters had gone to the club. My cousins and I were at the skating rink while they were at the night club.

On this particular weekend my aunt was responsible for picking us up from the skating rink, but she was running a little late. As we waited outside in the parking lot, a grey Nissan truck pulled up. Inside was a fair skin guy with a high top fade. I could instantly tell he was from the hood by the lean he had going. He introduced himself. He said, "They call me Mel, short for Melvin."

Mel had recently moved to Dallas from Houston along with his mother, brother, and two sisters. They all lived in a two bedroom apartment in Oak Cliff. Mel had a charming personality, was well known, and respected in the neighborhood.

We started to see each other rather often and Mel eventually asked me to be his girlfriend. I was very shy at the time and didn't talk much. Since I had no experience at this relationship thing, my conversation only consisted of about five words total. Yes, no, or I don't care. I was very simple, quiet, and conflict free.

Mel immediately started to spoil me with jewelry, the latest fashions, and always kept money in my pocket. I remember getting into his long Buick and going down to Big T Bazaar to pick up a new outfit to rock for the weekend. He liked for me to look good all the time, so he made sure I was well kept.

I never heard him mention a job nor did I ask what he did for a living. As time went on I figured it out. He would pull out huge bankrolls of money, folded with the large bills on top and held together by a thick rubber band. I would even see him ironing the money to get it straight and flat as possible. I really couldn't figure why this was necessary until after watching the movie New Jack City. In the movie the money taken in from drug sells was then ironed and counted in a money machine.

The Warning

During that summer his ex-girlfriend came to Dallas from Houston with their one year old daughter, Mai. She was now staying with Mel's family along with her daughter in this two bedroom apartment.

One weekend while over to his place, his mother and sister had gone out. It was Mel, Mai, his ex-girlfriend and me at the house alone. I stepped outside for a few minutes just to get some air. I was standing on the porch when I heard screams. It was a woman's voice coming from inside the house. I couldn't make out what was being said but quickly rushed back in to see what was going on. When I entered the bedroom I witnessed Mel landing his fist straight into his ex-girlfriend's face as if she was a guy. She was a small petite lady. By the looks of the hard blows Mel was throwing, I knew he had broken her jaw. I yelled for him to stop and began to pull him off of her. He stopped and stormed out of the house not saying a word.

The ex-girlfriend staggered to her feet holding her face as she said these words to me, "I'll give him three months and he'll be doing the same thing to you." In my mind when she began to speak I was prepared for something more like, "Thanks for helping me" or "I'm sorry you had to see this", but instead she was actually giving me a warning. My ears were still ringing from the screams she sirened out and I couldn't grasp an understanding of what just happened.

I knew for sure I couldn't take a punch like that and I immediately denied that dramatic scene. Thinking back it reminded me of a movie clip from, "What's Love Got to Do With It." Just pick a scene. There were several scenes capturing Ike's and Tina's love hate relationship. All I thought was, "No way, not me." Mel would never treat me like that. I didn't give him a reason to beat the slobber out of my mouth and force screams of mercy from my lungs. As I denied these actions ever happening, she reassured me they would indeed take place.

The Hint

It was Saturday night and as I stood in the doorway five feet tall weighing about a buck-five in a red spandex dress showing off all the curves while waiting for the rest of the crew to get dressed to head out. He didn't say much about the dress I had on, but he made it real clear he didn't want me to wear it ever again by his actions. Within a minute of him approaching me from behind, I started to feel a draft of air and then my straps began to fall from my shoulders. With one slice, he had split the dress down the back. I was speechless and pretty much naked as I hurried to get myself together.

As time went by, I could sense something was wrong. Mel didn't express himself much unless he was angry. So I didn't know for sure what was bothering him. I did know that things were not like they were in the beginning. The trips to the Bazaar had slowed down. He was no longer buying or doing things he used to for me. I never asked anything of him nor complained when things changed. But I could tell the lack of money bothered him and made him very irritated.

He became very jealous, insecure, and even paranoid at times. The abuse did start just as his ex-girlfriend said it would. It was so minor in the beginning. I really didn't compare it to what I had witnessed with his ex-girlfriend and pretty much thought nothing of it. It started out with him twisting my wrist, maybe a push or shove every now and then. He would twist my wrist so much until at one point my wrist was so sore, I could barely hold my own plate of food.

Episodes or The Way it is

Later on that summer, I was out with his sister, Trisha, at a club in South Dallas. It was a small joint, but the music was live and the people were having fun. We had a great time that night. I had been approached by a few guys who had given me their phone numbers.

Mel's sister Trisha was the coolest, so I thought. Just before dropping me off where Mel was, I remember her smiling with a slight giggle in her voice saying, "Girl let me hold those for you", and referring to the phone numbers I had gotten at the club. I didn't really understand what was happening or why she took the phone numbers, but I would soon find out.

As soon as I got in the house Mel began to drill me with questions. The questions were back to back as if he was a part of the FBI. I felt like I was a suspect on the First 48 inside the interrogation room with no where to run. It was not long after the questions stopped when he then ordered me to take off all my clothes. I hadn't done anything and didn't understand why I had to take off all my clothes. I looked at him with uncertainty on my face. He shouted again for me to take my clothes off. This time I could feel the intensity of his order and actually jumped from the out burst. I didn't waste any more time and immediately started to remove my clothes while trying hard to hold back my tears of shame.

He was upset and I wasn't sure why. I just did what he asked. Little did I know I was in a full blown strip-search. He was searching for phone numbers. He was like a crazy person.

I stood there naked and scared watching him cut the cord from a fan and then shave one end down to the wires. He then plugged the cord into the wall socket. I said nothing, not a word. I stood there still as a board, watching him make sparks fly from joining the wires together. His intension was to scare the hell out of me and all I can say, mission accomplished.

Again he questioned me starring me down with his eyes, taking slow steps toward me with the cord in his hand. While holding the cord close to my arm, I jumped as the sparks flew towards me. He threatened to electrocute me if I didn't tell him the truth. My mind racing, I begged for him to stop and reassured him I was telling the truth.

Despite the torture I had just gone through Mel and I remained together after that.

A Love Thang

One Saturday night I was hanging out with his sister and her boyfriend at Club Latrice on Martin Luther King, Jr. Boulevard. It wasn't long before Mel showed up. My fun was surely over and by the look on his face I knew it was time for me to go. When Mel pulled up he waved for me to get in the car. I was scared as hell and didn't want him to get upset. So without any hesitation I got in the car.

He continued to fuss and yell at me as we traveled South on Interstate 45. I had pretty much zoned his words out and was more focused on where we were headed thinking to myself, "Where are we going at this time of night?" Unsure and too scared to even breathe hard let alone ask him anything. We finally exited off the freeway and made a left turn travelling across the over-path. The roads were dark as a tunnel and very dusty. They had a spooky feeling that gave me the creeps. We were in a small country town outside of Dallas called Wilmer Hutchins.

We drove a bit before the car came to a slow rolling stop. I looked up and could barely make out my surroundings pass all the darkness. There were a few trees and some concrete stones about a few feet above the ground. My heart was pounding. We were in a graveyard.

He looked at me with a disturbed glare and told me this way he would know where to find me. I took a slow swallow and deep breath right before the tears streamed up and started to fill my eyes. I was motionless with an inside jerking shake, heart pounding with terror, and tears now running down my face trying to predict what's about to happen.

I apologized with a soft cry and begged to go home. We finally made it back to his place. Believe me, the drive home was long. Somehow, I had escaped another one of Mel's episodes of violence and personal death sentences.

I continued along in the relationship. A few weeks had passed since the last incident. His sister and I had gone to get some food to eat. Maybe we took too long. Again, I had no clue what was going on as usual. All I knew was that he was mad, again.

After getting out of the truck and walking towards his apartment, shots began to ring out. Someone was firing a gun and because of its ear deafening force, I couldn't tell where the shots were coming from. Trisha and I looked around to see where the shots were coming from when I noticed a man hanging out the window. It was Mel firing shots and aiming the gun at me.

I hurried into the house. Inside he began to shove me with his body pushing me into the bedroom. He pushed me down on the bed, sat on top of my stomach, and pointed the gun to the middle of my forehead. I closed my eyes for a moment and tried to get my thoughts together. I had experienced a lot of mental and emotional trauma many times before, but never with a gun in my face.

My face wet from the falling tears, I could feel the barrel of the gun pressing against my forehead. I pleaded for him to put the gun down. Then he turned the tables. He removed the gun from my head and placed it up against his chest. He forced me to grab the gun, while holding my hand and placing my finger on the trigger. I was shaking and crying uncontrollably. Images going through my mind of blood splatter as he put pressure on my finger causing a slow squeeze on the trigger. I had to do something quick.

I could barely talk from the nausea feeling in my throat but managed to mumble out the words, "I love you." I don't believe I had ever said those words before. I knew I had never said those words to a man for sure, but something in me forced them out. I really didn't even know what those words really meant. His reaction let me know they had power.

The room now calm, moving as the tension shifted. I felt the relief of a storm passing. Watching the tornado clouds move out and the sun shining through. Mel dropped the gun down onto the bed next to his leg. With his head down tears began to fall. He was crying and sobbing like a baby. This scene was getting weirder by the minute. He hadn't said much to me, so I didn't know what caused the episode. Plus, I had never seen him so vulnerable. I can only guess the words triggered a sense of belonging, maybe even a sense of unity that he strongly desired deep down inside, but was buried underneath the dope dealer lifestyle of hustling and his ego.

It Ain't Over

This was my first relationship and I didn't know what to expect, but I knew in my gut this relationship wasn't right. I began to distance myself from him by not going over to house and hoping he would find someone else or even better just forget about me. Mel had made it perfectly clear to me and everybody else in the neighborhood that I was his woman. I tried several times talking to him, which I thought people do in relationships when trying to fix their issues and make the relationship better. I finally got the nerve to tell him I didn't want to be with him anymore. Mel wasn't hearing it. I ended up picking myself up off the floor. Again he made it clear to me what I was in and that it wouldn't be that easy to leave with very little words said.

I had been away for a while when I got a call from Mel. I was at my mother's house when he telephoned with a creepy tone in his voice. It was similar to Liam Neeson in the movie "Taken", when he calls up the kidnappers and says, "I will find you", but Mel's words were, "It ain't over until I say it's over." He threatened to shoot up my mother's house and then hung up the phone.

After that call I didn't waste any time. I had seen some of his work on the streets, so I knew he was more than capable and willing to follow through with what he said. I packed up a few of my belongings and left.

I had met a guy name Joe and after telling him my situation he offered to let me stay with him. That same night, Mel shot up my mother's house.

My Cry

I was out with Joe's roommate's girlfriend telling her how I had met Joe and about the last relationship I had just got out of. I shared with her a few incidents I had gone through with Mel. Her face was stunned with disbelief of the stories and all the drama.

We pulled up at a nearby 7-Eleven off of Illinois and Corinth street still having a conversation about Mel when a car drove up beside us. A man jumped out of his car and approached the passenger window. It almost seemed like I was seeing things. I couldn't believe my eyes. I screamed, she screamed. Our lungs were rumbling with screams of fear, our hearts were racing, and our bodies shaking. It was Mel. I yelled, "Go, go, go". She hit reverse and spun out of the parking lot, driving as if we were running from New York's finest. Forget about stop signs- she flew right pass every last one. Now I wasn't sure if I was screaming because we were being chased or of her reckless driving. She sped down the wrong side of the road, hitting curves on two wheels like she had just taken a crash course from Paul and Tyrese in "Fast and the Furious".

Joe's house was about three minutes from the 7-Eleven store where we were. We got to the house in about 45 seconds flat. When we pulled to Joe's house, she had barely put the car in park when all I seen were her feet flying, as she ran into the house. She had jumped out and left me in the car. I knew help was coming, and then I realized Joe had already left for work. Mel was dead on our heels. When we pulled up, so did he. Before I could get both feet on the ground Mel was pulling up on my side of the car. I didn't even have a chance to run. I just knew the police would come shortly, so I tried to stall hoping someone would come out to help me. Mel was yelling at me, "Get out the car," looking like an angry Rottweiler from the other side of the car window. I proceeded to unlock the door, but when he would grab the door handle, I would quickly lock the door back. This made him very mad. After few times Mel became very pissed and began hitting the window with his fist yelling for me to get out of the car. As the blows to the glass became harder I decided it was best for me to get out of the car before he comes through the window to get me.

I was hardly out of the car into an upright stand when I felt the blows to my head. Mel was hit me with his pistol across my head and pushed me in the car. I felt like a little child that had just gotten in trouble and was being disciplined by her parent, but he wasn't my parent.

We drove down Illinois to some apartments not too far from where we were. Mel's friend sat in the back seat quietly. Once Mel went into the apartment he said, "I already knew what was going to happen when we saw you. Why don't you just move out of town or somewhere?" I didn't know what was going to happen next, but I knew I wanted out.

I know for sure God heard my silent prayer I said as we drove up Illinois Road after leaving the apartments. It wasn't long before the police pulled us over. I was relieved to see those lights flashing as they instructed us to pull over, but Mel wasn't. He had tickets, so he was arrested. After handcuffing him and putting him in the car I told the officer what had happened earlier that day and also about the shooting. One of the officers escorted me back to my mom's house. I pointed out the bullet holes that Mel had left from the shooting a few weeks earlier.

Even though Mel had been arrested, the fear and torture still lived in me. For years I had nightmares and anxiety attacks just from talking about those horrible experiences which are common for people who have been traumatized.

Violence in teen dating

I met Mel during my 8th grade year in middle school. Mel was only 17 years old. Studies show that 1 in 5 teens will encounter violence in teen dating. Children exposed to abuse in their home are more likely to encounter abuse in their relationships as they perceive this to be normal. The first signs of abuse are usually so unnoticeable you may over look them as an accident or playful joking such as choking, twisting the arm or wrist, pushing or being pinned down. All the extra attention may come off as cute yet is more of a possessive ownership character and can be mistaken for love. Because of the embarrassment abuse brings, teens will not ask for help from family and friends and may even hide the abuse. Each year nearly 10% of high school students are victims of dating violence.

> **Red flags** to look for in teens to know if they are _dating an abuser_ or _may be an abuser_:
> 1. Has a history of violence and/or threats use of violence
> 2. Extremely jealous
> 3. Constantly checks up on you
> 4. Controlling behavior
> 5. Isolates you from your family and friends
> 6. Gets upset if he sees you looking at someone else
> 7. Quick tempered
> 8. Bullying
> 9. Aggressive
> 10. Blames others for their problems
> 11. Humiliates or belittles you
> 12. Abuses animals

A low love tank from neglect or the absence of the father often leaves a child feeling unloved in which they seek to fill this void by finding replacement from a person that gives them this missed attention. It is the parents' job to teach their teenagers the importance of self-worth and self love. Teenagers who value themselves won't need to "find themselves" in other people.

In dating relationships, 1 in 5 adolescent girls are victims of physical or sexual abuse or both.

> **Red flags** to look for in teens to know if they *are being victimized*:
> 1. Depression
> 2. Mood swings
> 3. Isolation from family members and friends
> 4. Urgent need to communicate with boyfriend
> 5. Low performance in school
> 6. Difficulty in making decisions
> 7. Need for approval of a boyfriend before making decisions
> 8. Unexplained physical injuries.

Establishing and maintaining a strong communication between the parent and the teen, cultivates healthy dating attitudes and respectful relationships. Most importantly, enforce and develop zero tolerance of any form of dating violence. Dating and domestic violence is linked to the abuser witnessing or experiencing violence themselves. Some youth believe that love and abuse go together. Victims of dating violence often make excuses for the individual and do not realize that this behavior is not acceptable or normal.

Spouse abuse in adulthood is 10 times more likely by boys who witnessed their fathers' violence than boys from non-violent homes.

Love is kind.

If you're a teen and involved in an abusive relationship, please report it to your parents, school officials, police, or security guard.

Parents please listen to your children and encourage them to talk about the abuse. No one deserves to be abused. Abuse is a very serious matter. For help with addressing and coping with abuse, contact your local abuse hotline, social service agencies, and churches, which may have additional resources like support groups for victims of abuse.

NOTES

My First Love

CHAPTER THREE

Same Guy Different Name

I'm a victim. I'm helpless. I was in a constant wait to be rescued. I'm damaged and I can't seem to make a relationship work. This is the story I told myself and it manifested into life. I had labeled myself and was wearing the sign on my forehead that said, "I like pain, please give me a good dose." I was comfortable with being the child victim receiving the much needed attention through angry outburst of rage followed by remorse. I felt special, but in a dysfunctional way. It was really a false perception of love and fondness that cost me my soul.

During the spring of 2014 I ran across a well keep secret. The news was shocking to my ears. I had stumbled upon a video by Napoleon Hill filmed in black and white. Napoleon Hill spoke about the Law of Attraction. He explained how everything in our lives we attract whether it is good or bad; positive or negative. I started to think back over all the things that happened to me and the people included in these events. I was a miserable person. Pretty much everything that came from my mouth was negative. My past pain was the primary focus and therefore I continued to create more of it. I created more **Pain**.

The Victim

At a night club in North Dallas, a dark skinned and stocky guy approached me and called me out by my nickname. With a puzzled look on my face, I stared at him trying to recollect where I knew him from, but nothing came to mind. He asked, "You don't remember me?" Staring at him with an unsure look, I shook my head responding, "NO." A feeling of uneasiness covered my body as he told me about where I worked and other personal information he knew about me. I didn't know this man. I had never seen him before, had no interest in him and really wanted him to leave me alone. He offered me his number and told me to give him a call. I wasn't interested in him, and I didn't have the guts to tell him no thanks, so I took his number just so he would leave me alone.

A few weeks had gone by and I decided to go out to a local bar. You wouldn't believe I ran into this same guy again. With a glad to see you smile on his face, he began to ask me why I hadn't called. He pleaded with me about letting him take me out. In my mind a man with this kind of persistence, I thought he must be really interested, so why not give him try. I had that gut instinct the whole time about this guy, but excused it with his determination.

You see I had been targeted. I gave off all of the right signals. I was
- a care giver who felt valued when I fixed things
- a people pleaser with a history of being used
- timid and unassertive
- responsible and blamed myself for any problems that occurred
- felt like I deserved bad things to happen
- felt special from all the negative attention
- familiar with living with an angry person
- weak and had a hard time making decisions for myself
- playing out the victim role and did not demand anything
- only looking for the good in people, overlooking their problems

For our first date, Blair wanted to take me to a party coming up in Tyler, Texas in a few weeks. It sounded fun, so I agreed to go. When the weekend came for us to go the party he informed me that it would be too late for us to drive back home the same night. He suggested I bring a change of clothes and we would return on that Sunday. On the way down he had some pretty decent conversation to make the time go by, we stopped for dinner, and then picked up some liquor to get the party started early. We had a great time at the club. I even saw an old friend so I was really glad I came.

When we got back to the hotel I was pretty tipsy from the alcohol and was ready to just pass out on the bed. But Blair had another plan. I had just met him and hadn't even thought about having sex with him. However, sex was heavy on his mind. He made passes at me and I rejected them several time. Shortly after telling him no the last time and trying to roll over, he forced himself on top of me. With his shoulders pressed on top of my arms he began to remove my clothes. I tried to push him off of me, but it didn't work. He was much stronger and his body weight made it hard for me to even breathe.

I felt stupid and disappointed with myself for even coming along on this trip. After he was finished, he had the nerve to ask me was it good as if I had made some type of gesture that I wanted to have sex with him. I rolled my eyes at him and tried to go to sleep.

Long Nights

I excused Blair's actions and continued to see him after this incident. I was living with a relative at the time and mentioned to him that I needed to find another place to stay. He immediately went out to get an apartment. My son, Blair and I had moved into this apartment together.

A few weeks had passed since we moved. One Friday night Blair had gone out. I tried to reach him by phone but he didn't answer. I had left a few messages on his voicemail and had waited for him to call me back. But he never called. Thoughts of him with another woman filled my mind. Now I was really mad and had gone as far as locking the top lock of the door so he couldn't get in when he did come home. After hours of waiting I fell asleep. It was the loud banging coming from outside the patio window that woke me. It was him. He had picked up a large object and was trying to get in through the balcony. He continued to throw the object against the window trying to break the glass, and he did just that. I got up and played asleep in the closet. When he got in he found me in the closet lying down. I felt his body standing behind me as I laid on the floor. He didn't say anything. He turned around and left out the door.

One Saturday night after leaving the club headed down Loop 12 to drop my friend off at home Blair called my cell phone. I was known for being a smarty pants and talking real fly at the mouth, which did not work in my favor that night. I was talking pretty off the wall and remembered repeating back to him saying, "You better have your boxing gloves on." I was only joking and had no clue what he was even talking about when I repeated it; we didn't even have any boxing gloves.

When I arrived and entered the house I took off my hat that I was wearing and placed it on the table. Blair had made it home before me. Within seconds he approached me with several punches to my face out of nowhere and then passed out on the bed. When I rose to my feet, the skirt I was wearing was twisted around my waist, my hair looked like it just went through a wind tunnel, and my face swollen from where he had hit me. I couldn't believe what had just happened and the fact that he was bold enough to fall asleep as if nothing had taken place. In my side view was a tall standing fan we had in our bedroom. I wanted him to feel pain like he had just given to me, but I knew my tiny hands would only make him laugh. So, I picked up the fan and knocked him across the head with it. What did I do this for? He woke up like a mad man throwing punches in midair as if he was in a boxing ring with Sugar Ray.

I had to call in sick to work a few days until my face had healed. When I looked in the mirror at myself I felt shamed and ugly, but yet I saw a familiar face. I had seen this person before in a movie growing up. This movie had a woman with a face that had been badly beaten, blood running from her forehead, crying and shaking -sitting quietly on the floor. This movie starring actress was my mother.

Blair apologized the next day for his actions. He looked remorseful and hurt about what happen as I did, so the relationship continued.

Controlling

We had plans to go out for dinner and then go over to the club. I pulled a few items from the closet looking for something to wear and couldn't make up my mind. I had pulled out a blue jean skirt with splits up the sides and decided to put it on. I thought it was cute and classy, but Blair didn't like it. He suggested I wear another similar black dress with the splits up the side. We went back and forward about the skirt. I didn't understand why he wanted me to change when they were so much alike. I was feeling like he was controlling me and I didn't like it. So, I didn't change my skirt. What was the big deal anyway? He came back in the room to check to see if I was ready. When he saw I had on the blue jean skirt he got upset. At this point I could care less about the clothes or the dinner, so I laid down in the bed with all my clothes on. I didn't want to fight. As a matter of fact, I didn't even want to go. I laid as still and quiet as possible not to cause any conflict. Blair approached the side of the bed and stood over me. With one strong grip and a blink he had snatched my skirt off of me and was now holding it in his hand. He had ripped it right off me as I lay in the bed. Still I didn't flinch or make a sound. A few minutes passed and I felt something in my gut that made me feel something wasn't right. It was really quiet, too damn quiet.

I went in the living room to see if he was still in the house. The living room was foggy. I could barely see. In the kitchen was an indoor campout. My skirt was the main part of the blazing fire. I immediately thought, "I better get the hell out of here." The kitchen was being consumed with so much smoke I started to cough and choke. As I headed for the front door, leaving out of the kitchen, I

saw him just sitting there on the couch calmly as if he was waiting on his Sunday dinner to be served. The fire was now covering the stove and I panicked. With no skirt on half naked, I headed straight for the front door. He grabbed me and wouldn't let me leave. He told me to stay in here and "take it!" The fire was still blazing from the stove. The smoke alarm siren was loud. I coughed hard choking from the smoke. I knew I was going to die that night.
How much more?

Cruel Punishment

I met a guy and he had invited me out to karaoke night on Friday. I knew Blair had other women and would be gone, so I agreed to go. I told Blair I was meeting my cousins and that we were having a girls' night out. I had a great time listening to people sing their hearts out infused with alcohol to get their courage up. As the guy walked me out he asked me was I ready to go home. I wasn't. We sat in his truck and talked. As I was explaining to him about my living situation, Blair called and I answered. I let him know we were leaving and would be home shortly. He called back again, but I didn't answer. He called several times. I continued my conversation about the abuse and how unhappy I was when the phone rang again. I must have accidently hit the answer button because upon getting out of the truck I noticed the call time was way over ten minutes. I was unsure what Blair had heard. Had this date fallen through?

The apartment was jet black and cold. When I turned on the lights I noticed the phone line had been cut and the phone smashed. It was it if I was in a screen from a horror movie. I could feel something was about to happen and probably should have left at this point. I entered the bedroom and there he was. His energy was calm and focused. He looked me in the face and asked who I was with. I stuck to the story of being with my cousins at the club. He moved closer to me and asked who the guy I was talking to was. I told him he was a friend and we were only talking about you. He was fuming with a calm rage.

A couple of weeks earlier he had punched me in the mouth. With blood running from my face I yelled at him "Don't put your hands on me again." He agreed not to hit me anymore. Little did I know it was not the end of the abuse.

Blair went into the restroom and grabbed a bottle and began to drench my clothes with liquid. I stood there dismayed watching the liquid fly from the bottle and drench my clothes. Him drawing back his arm until the bottle had nothing left in it. His face in a still lock position, his eyes empty just like the bottle. I asked, "What are you doing?" As the bottle of aftershave hit the floor, he replied, "I told you I wasn't going to hit you anymore." He then turned and walked over and grabbed a small box. With every step while looking me dead in my eyes, he began to strike one match at a time and fling them towards my feet. I couldn't think; I was paralyzed. I remember saying to myself, "Lord make this stop."

After torching me with matches he grabbed a wire hanger and grabbed me around my neck. He began to take off my pants mumbling. "You're not going to want to have sex with anyone else." I shouted at him, "I didn't do anything." He folded the wire hanger the long way. I had heard back in the day of women using wire hangers to induce a miscarriage, but I wasn't pregnant. I kicked and screamed trying to free myself from this monster. Tears rolling down my eyes, I was getting tired and short of breath. I managed to get the words out, "I love you." Still praying to myself, "Lord make this stop." Blair wasn't trying to hear me. He shouted, "Don't try to tell me you love me now."

I had finally got the strength and courage to leave Blair. Abusers usually apologize following the abuse, reassuring that it will not happen again. This is only temporary and as soon as they are under pressure they will shift back to violence. Even though I had left him, and we were no longer in a relationship, he still came by my mother's house to harass me threatening to burn down the house. Sometimes called all night long and I mean it was all damn night long to the point I would have to turn off the ringer. Sadly, I could still hear the phone ringing in my head because it had rung so much.

Leaving a domestic violence relationship can be a very dangerous step to take. Women are often perceived as property and the abuser will go to great means to keep control even to killing her.

Control being the main purpose of abuse. Setting fear in the victim gives the abuser the power needed to sustain their control. It is said that 1 in 4 women will experience abuse in their life time.

Similar to a child molester who grooms their victim prior to the act to gain trust, so does the violent abusers. They have such a great need to feel in control often from their own lack of control and feeling powerless as a child.

A Familiar Place

I finally realized the familiarity of these relationships. One common factor in most abuse cases were the passive, uninvolved or absentee father. Secondly, the love I received from these men was usually linked to gifts and other items followed by betrayal. I witnessed this kind of love before as a child. This gave me the since of familiar or normalcy. The love that was cultivated was toxic and was destroying me from the inside out.

Being the victim is easy and sometimes even comfortable because of being familiar with the role. It only takes a decision to make the change that could result in life or death.

My relationships were usually a poor match from the beginning. The red flags were waving in my face but I walked right passed them. Looking back, I can see the pattern. The relationships would start off really great overloaded with gifts and kind acts of service, followed by a test to see if I would accept the abuse that is to come, and then gifts and kindness would fade away with the increase of abuse over time. Finally after I had taken so much abuse I would leave. Then enter into a new relationship and repeat the cycle.

I made the decision to give my children a different movie to look at and no longer remain a victim of life, but take charge of my life and live it to the fullest. I took actions to identify the root of my problem, discover ways to use my mess as a stepping stone, and implement healthy boundaries that transformed my life.

Abuse causes mental, emotional, spiritual, and physical damage. Each area requires attention to properly heal. During my journey I wanted a speedy recovery. After one counseling session and a prayer I expected to wake up whole and free of the nightmares. There are no quick fixes. It takes time to transform, heal, and renew what has been taken, damaged, and altered. But it is in that process you uncover the person buried beneath the tears.

NOTES

Same Guy Different Name

CHAPTER FOUR

Healing

In my world of consumed negativity and humiliation, it seemed as if no one loved me. Love, earned by the hard work of gathering points of approval and acceptance while dancing to someone else's tune was a daily routine for me. Even if the music made my ears hurt from the agonizing sound of manipulation or caused me physical pain, I worked even harder to gain the admiration certificate of approval that would expire upon completing the task.

"People Pleaser", an acquired role of never ending discontentment to please, having hope of one day in return to be loved by all. I had taken on this role as a young girl. I was praised for being quiet and not causing much conflict. I even had a nickname, "Good Girl".

A day came when I grew weary of trying and attempting this unreachable level of certainty; that I was liked or loved. After years and years of working in a position that was surely a dead-end, I realized there was another side of me. It was a side that would surface every now and then, mostly to take care of the *real* business. This side I called "Bad Girl", she didn't hesitate, or care in the moment if she had to raise her voice, or become angry to get her point across. She was fearless.

However, it wasn't long afterwards, "Bad Girl" would feel shameful of her actions.

Conflict of Interest

Why didn't "Bad Girl" show up more often? Why did "Good Girl" only allow her to come out at certain times and for only a short period of time? These were the questions I asked myself.

"Good Girl" wanted full control of my life and only allowed "Bad Girl" to come out when things were a total mess or had an immediate need to be rescued.

In my chaos of conflict, I discovered the rescuer I had desperately sought out since childhood was present the whole time. The rescuer was ME. For some reason I felt bad or shameful after letting "Bad Girl" come out. A sense of uneasiness would arise that reminded me that this behavior was not one of a lady.

These thoughts kept my emotions and behavior in total conflict and chaos. There were days I would even say to myself, "Maybe I should check myself into the psychiatric ward," it was just that bad. There was a battle going on inside of me between "Good Girl" and

"Bad Girl", of who would win. Good Girl was always winning with her dominate character and drive to **please**, only to call on Bad Girl to bail her out. But, the strange thing about this whole clashing of character was I needed both. I needed balance.

Greatest Love of All

During elementary school while waiting in the auditorium for our teachers to arrive, Principal Allen would play a song by Whitney Houston, "The Greatest Love of All". I can still hear it playing loudly like it was yesterday. At that age I didn't quite understand the message the song conveyed or the intention of the principal for playing the same song *every* morning. Ironically, the elementary school was in a low income area filled with violence, poverty, alcohol, substance abuse, single mothers, and teenage pregnancy.

"The Greatest Love of All" was written by Michael Masser and Linda Creed. Creed at that time wrote the lyrics during her struggle with breast cancer in 1977 and the song was later popularized by Whitney Houston in 1985. The words describing Creed's feelings of coping with life's greatest challenges, whether you succeed or fail, and instructing you to find that inner love that is easy to achieve and yet the greatest love of all.

Today, I totally understand the message from the lyrics. If I had to sum it up I would say, "Self love is the greatest love of all." Learn to love you despite your environment, trauma, neglect, abandonment, negative comments and the strange faces people make at you. Love every inch of you.

It is not until you truly love yourself that love finds you in every area of your life.

Awakening

After years of blaming myself for what happened, I grew tired and weary. I was sick of my life and my self destructive behavior. I was desperate and way past sick and tired. I was disgusted with my life. The heavy drinking, sleeping pills, gambling, over eating, jumping jobs, codependent relationships, mismanagement of money, and moving had taken its toll. I wanted something better, not just for me, but for my children as well. So, I did the only thing I hadn't tried, I cried out to God. I had tried everything else and it didn't work. So, I tried God's way.

I mean I yelled, slung tears and snot until I was exhausted. From the outside of the room, you would have thought there was a gang of five in the room from the racket I was keeping up. On that same day, I was delivered from my chronic drinking and the self-medication I had implemented to help me sleep and cope with my past. I drank to the point that at times I wouldn't make it home or I would fall asleep with my foot on the brake of my car, while waiting in line at a drive thru. I was going to self destruct or kill someone else in the process. Something had to change.

I made up my mind to stop this cycle of destruction. The cycle of abuse had been deeply rooted and planted in all the women of my family, all of whom at some point in their lives had experienced abuse and even passed it on to their children.

I didn't want my daughter to walk in the house with a black eye or get a phone call from her with news she had been betrayed or mistreated by someone she loved. So, at this point I had to change.

I began to pray on a consistent basis to God. Asking Him to remove the spirit of depression, the spirit of anxiety, to break the curse that was upon my family, to give me the strength and the courage to heal, courage to stand up for myself, and the courage to love. As time went on I no longer required the normal sleep aids in order to sleep through the night. My sleep became so peaceful. Free from worry. I felt like a new born baby, safe and protected while resting in her father's arms.

I Forgave

I've come to realize that acknowledgement plays a major part in the healing process, facing the fact that it did happen. To come to grips with self and honestly say this is not right. I didn't deserve to be beaten, yelled at, or mistreated. And it wasn't my fault. I forgave myself after years of hating and blaming myself for the abuse. I even attempted suicide at the age of 17 and thought about it several times in my twenties to end the pain I carried with me. I was stuck in the denial stage; failing to acknowledge any wrongdoing of the abusers and trying to drown out my own hurt and pain with alcohol and partying.

It was Sunday morning around 7:00 am, my mind still puzzled about what it meant to be a woman, the events that had occurred, my purpose, and life itself. I was sitting at my desk when I received the message. I had prayed with a friend a few days before, asking God for clarity about my life. In the prayer, we asked for a "jolt awakening" so the message would be so clear I wouldn't have any doubt about the message.

I was in the middle of completing this book when I heard the soft whispers of wisdom. It was as if someone had whispered to me words of magic. In a lower tone of voice, I repeated the words to myself a few times. Then it hit me, I jumped up out of my seat as if I had just witnessed Michael Jordan slam dunk the ball with 3 seconds left on the clock to win the championship game.

I shouted, "I got it, I got it!" I was still carrying the label *abused, handle with care*.

The message was, "Take off the label." It was an invisible label that I wore engraved on my forehead after experiencing abuse. It was similar to a company marking "damaged goods" with a red stamp on a product that no longer measured up to standard.

The message simply implied for me to stop labeling myself because I was now restored and made *new*. Forgive yourself and take off the label.

Self-Acceptance

It was shortly after sunrise when I felt compelled to go to the bathroom. Normally, I would look in the mirror and shock myself from the smeared eye makeup followed by harsh words to start my day. I would make statements to myself like, "you look horrible", "nobody wants a woman with a morning face like that", or something along those lines. But this particular day I stared in the mirror at this woman puzzled and curious about whom she was.

Her life story displayed years of ups and downs, she put on a few extra pounds, hair mangled, but her eyes still big and bright and filled with the wonder of a child.

I stood up straight, facing the mirror, chin up, and hands on my hips looking eye to eye with this woman and said, "I love you." She didn't seem moved by those words of affection, so I repeated them again. "I love you." Her cheeks raised as her eyes began to tear up slightly. She smiled with approval and began her day. It was a day of self-acceptance of my own value, my experiences, my good and bad sides, and love I added to the world.

If you are reading this book and have experienced physical or sexual abuse, I want you to personally know, you did nothing to deserve that type of treatment. I am so sorry for the pain you endured and pray for your healing.

How to Get Past the Pain

Get rid of all bitterness, rage, and anger, brawling and slander, along with every form of malice. Be kind and compassionate to one another, forgiving each other, just as Christ God forgave you.
– Ephesians 4:31-32

Seek Professional Help

I was probably on my third session when the therapist suggested we create an x-ray. This would not be your ordinary medical x-ray where you go into the x-ray room, throw on that heavy 25 pound jacket, and stand in front of a machine. This was an x-ray of my soul, looking for the emotional damage. There isn't a machine capable of measuring or detecting heartache, but we were on a mission to find the poison that filled my veins. The therapist had instructed me to write down each occurrence that caused me emotional pain, and to identify the emotion associated with it along with my age at the time of the event. From this information, I created a board with a small circle in the middle. This circle represented my true self. I drew circles around my false self. Each circle growing larger and larger, attaching *labels* to the emotional pain associated with each event. Needless to say, I ran out of room on my board as the number of circles increased and filled the board. Right in front of my eyes, layer on top of layer, year after year of neglect disappointment, worthlessness, unappreciated, betrayal, sadness, abandonment, and loneliness laid all stretched out on the board. My true self had been covered up by the events in my life and the person I presented myself to be was really my false self. My false self-presented a character of shyness, timidity, simpleness, quiet, non-risk taker, non-expressive, a loner, isolated, and emotionally numb to love and affection. We had managed to dig up my true self, a person much more alive and exciting. We dug her out from underneath all the rubble, a buried treasure waiting to be discovered.

Detox

Healing takes place in three different areas: physical, mental, and spiritual. As part of my physical healing I purchased the Dherb Full Body cleanse, a 20 day herbal-based cleansing system designed to cleanse the body from head to toe. In my unhappiness, I turned to food. Some foods I even developed an emotional attachment to that I associated great pleasure with when ever eaten. My eyes would light up and suddenly increase my heart rate with just the mention of these foods. A detox was definitely needed.

Reading

Did you know 80% of the population grew up in a dysfunctional environment? Reading and learning about abuse gave me a better understanding about my life and the events that had taken place. Reading helped me to put closure on my pain, but in no way did it excuse what happened.

Books are like gold to me. They hold stories of wisdom, knowledge, basic principles, how-to processes, and philosophy that could and can change your life. The more I read, the more of the child-like imagination came back. Books gave me the opportunity to dream and imagine again. Something I hadn't done since I was a very young child. Books awakened my intellectual side, allowed me to tap into new possibilities, dream, imagine, and explore a whole new world through the eyes of others.

Meditate

I've had enough excitement already to last a lifetime. There's no need in me going to see the movie, "50 Shades of Grey". All I wanted was peace. Participating in a twenty-one day emotional cleanse really helped clear my emotional channels. I strongly had the desire to heal and move from the emotionless state of being I was in. Most importantly, I wanted to love. I wanted to remove the walls that blocked people out of my life or caused me to run from relationships. Meditation allows time for you to quiet the mind and hear your innermost, deepest thoughts and desires. For me, the real transformation did not take place in the outside world. You see, the real transformation took place by the renewing of my mind. My mind kept re-living hurtful events, kept me in fear, and reproduced the feelings of abandonment, loneliness, and worthlessness when certain situations reminded me of my past. Meditation allowed time for me to tap into these areas and address each of them head on. It brought awareness and taught me how to live in the present.

Exercise

Get moving. Exercise has many great benefits. Exercising helps to stimulate the brain while working out the physical body. Exercise is also known to improve your mood, reduce stress, relieve anxiety, increase self-confidence, and boost your energy levels.

Journal

Journaling are those snap shoots of your life that you capture and go back to review later to clarify your thoughts; you get to know yourself better; resolve disagreements with others; reflect or process events, and track your progress. For me I used a simple notebook at first, writing down hurtful events, relationship patterns, and even some of the foods I ate that gave emotional pleasure but my body didn't seem to agree with. I believe it was reading all the negative miserable stories over and over that really gave me the motivation to create a better life.

Journaling is a strategy to get your thoughts out and help bring awareness of habits and patterns by putting them down on paper. It's also another stress reliever and a good place to park your emotional tantrums.

Practice Forgiveness

Forgiveness is a decision to **release** yourself from the hurt and anger, so you no longer hold on to it and let it destroy you. What happened hurt, but it doesn't have to hurt the rest of your life. Making a decision to forgive does not excuse their behavior, but allows you to release the anger, resentment, and bitterness in your heart, so you can move forward. Forgiveness is responding to the hurt, releasing yourself from the emotional prison and starting the process to restore peace and bring balance to your life.

I dedicated some time to writing down the names of the people who had wronged me or hurt me in some way. Alone in a room I sat quietly on the floor and openly forgave all of them. It felt as if a diesel truck had just been lifted off my shoulders. It's funny how we think being angry at someone for a long periods of time will hurt them, but the truth is it really only hurts you. I had held on to my anger for over 32 years and finally gave myself permission to move on. I felt like a new person. I was a new person. My true self slowly started to return. I had been buried underneath all those negative events. I worked hard to unlock the door to the invisible jail that had me chained to a life of sabotage, anger, misery, resentment, complaining, failure, and defeat. I was now finally free and on my way to discover life.

> *"You have heard the law that says, 'Love your neighbor and hate your enemy.' But I say, love your enemies! Pray for those who persecute you!"* (Matthew 5:43-44, *NLT*)

Create New Memories

Healing from abuse is difficult especially in the beginning. The mind constantly tries to figure why things played out the way they did, searching for answers. I wanted to forget the past as fast as I could. The truth is you don't forget. I found exploring new things, finding out what makes you laugh, what other foods you enjoy, music, and exploring new places and traveling were opportunities to create new memories. New memories that eventually overshadowed the nightmares.

Learn to Love You

Since I had managed to shape my world of unworthiness around loveless acts, I too inflicted abusive behavior towards myself at times.

I was working from home one evening and noticed a mistake I made on a document. Without hesitation, putting emphasis on the "st" I said to myself, "now that's stupid!" I said it so loud I surprised my own self and looked around to make sure no one else was in the room listening. Luckily I was alone. I began to question why I would even say such a thing and recalled a time in my childhood when I was called stupid for making a not wise decision. I often replayed the memory of this event, which kept the moment fresh in my mind. Even though I had only been called "stupid" maybe once, I replayed the statement hundreds of times in my mind. I affirmed this toxic behavior with every negative thought or words I spoke to myself that kept the lie alive.

I had adopted and learned destructive behavior and was curious to find out what would happen if I replaced the destructive with a more positive, loving behavior. Instead of seeking love from the outside in, I implemented and affirmed self love from the inside out. My own self-worth was discovered during my spiritual journey. I took a deep look on the inside and recorded my discoveries on note cards. In the beginning I felt like a complete liar. Every morning I would reach in my nightstand drawer and pull out a stack of note cards. I noted several short affirmations such as, *"You're loveable"*, *"Don't put yourself at the bottom of the list"*, *"People love your spirit"*, and *"Don't be so hard on yourself, you did a good job."* The words were foreign to my ears and even made me uncomfortable but I continued to re-enforce them everyday. I began to be kind to myself, take time out for me, moving away from self-sabotaging behaviors.

Learn to Express Yourself

How many excuses have you used in order to stay in your comfort zone? What goals have you set for yourself? How many times have you allowed others to tell you what you can and cannot do? Many times I used plenty of excuses to keep myself comfortable, in fear of the unknown.

He Loves Me Not

I can give one good example; not applying for that position that I really wanted and was well qualified for. All along I was telling myself, "I didn't have enough experience, I didn't have a degree in that area, they probably have a lot of people applying, or they would never hire me anyways." These were all excuses I used to stay in my comfort zone, but deep inside knowing I should just go for it. Often when we are not telling ourselves what we "can't" do, we take on opinions of others. Doing what others feel we should be doing, placing a limit on our lives. I know this was true for me for a while, but as time went by it came to me that these were just that, opinions.

Put on those colorful shoes that really don't go with your outfit, take that trip, taste that funny looking food that everyone frowns at when you mention the name of it, or start that business you've been dreaming about. There are no limits but the ones you put on yourself.

Healing

Checklist of what love isn't

You have the choice of choosing how you want to be treated. To help avoid entering into an abusive relationship, use this list to help you identify and sort out what love is and what love isn't. Create a list of boundaries for yourself. Remember, people do what you *allow* them to do.

- ❏ Enjoyment
- ❏ Caring
- ❏ Pain
- ❏ Possessiveness
- ❏ Unkindness
- ❏ Getting pregnant
- ❏ Fear
- ❏ Friendship
- ❏ Respect
- ❏ Closeness
- ❏ Helplessness
- ❏ Strong positive feelings
- ❏ Trust
- ❏ Jealousy
- ❏ Obsession
- ❏ Selfish
- ❏ Forceful
- ❏ Proving yourself
- ❏ Openness
- ❏ Respecting differences
- ❏ Communication
- ❏ Violence
- ❏ Needy
- ❏ Sharing
- ❏ Honesty
- ❏ Manipulation
- ❏ Expecting all your needs to be met
- ❏ Forced Commitment
- ❏ Compromising
- ❏ Rage

Checklist of Symptoms Associated with Depression

Do you experience:
- ❑ Helplessness
- ❑ Discouragement
- ❑ Bothered and irritated by other people
- ❑ Unhappiness or emptiness
- ❑ Insignificance
- ❑ Unable to focus
- ❑ Uncompleted projects
- ❑ Indecisiveness
- ❑ Feel life will not get any better
- ❑ Loss of self-esteem
- ❑ Fatigue
- ❑ Repeated thoughts of suicide
- ❑ Trouble falling or staying asleep
- ❑ Loss of energy
- ❑ Feeling exhausted

The symptoms above are not to diagnose yourself, but to inform you of common symptoms found in individuals suffering with depression. You should seek professional help to assist you if you are experiencing feelings of depression. I am in no way suggesting medicate yourself in order to feel better. I am suggesting you seek

Healing

a professional counselor or therapist to have a guided conversation with you to get to the core cause of depression.

Post-Traumatic Stress Disorder

Loud, sudden noises would literally send me running. The nightmares and constant reminders of my past would trigger suicidal thoughts.

I jumped up one Sunday evening from a deep sleep. I saw a man standing over my bed. I tried to get myself together and went to the kitchen to get a glass of water. I gasped for air. It felt as if someone had a strong grip around my neck and was squeezing the air out of me. I couldn't breathe. I took in deep breaths trying to get some air in my lungs as tears filled my eyes because of the severe pain that came from the tightening of my chest. I thought I was having a heart attack. It turns out it was anxiety.

Post-Traumatic Stress Disorder develops as a result of events similar to survivors of war trauma. It can prevent people from building good relationships, interfere with work performance, and stop them from following through with other tasks. Instead, apply these events as a source of strength which will enable you to move from *victim* to **victor**.

Victims May Experience:

Depression
Reliving the event
Detachment
Anxiety

- Panic attacks
- Stress
- Sleep disturbances
- Flashbacks or dreams of event
- Fear
- Anger
- Grief
- Feeling stuck
- Shock
- Suicidal thoughts

Choose to Live

Forgiving oneself and breaking the silence chases away the pain and shame. Remember, you survived. Commit to healing and moving past the pain. *I no longer choose to live in the past.* I have accepted the things that happened in my past knowing I cannot change what took place.

Trust me, I know this is way easier said than done, but you must also forgive the people that hurt you, betrayed you, neglected you, and abandoned you. Will it take work? YES it will. But, it is very well worth having a life filled with joy versus a life filled with sadness, resentment, and bitterness.

My pain led me down a path of darkness. However, there was light at the end of the tunnel teaching me of great deal of what I know today. In my traumatic experience of abuse were also my gifts of compassion and empathy for others. This journey has not been an easy road to travel. But I continue on because I want something more for me, something for me to share with others.

Each of us has something good to offer the world. We must discover what that is.

Healing

NOTES

He Loves Me Not

CHAPTER FIVE

Self-Esteem

Abuse diminishes your self-esteem. The black eye or busted lip you have to wear in public can cause a great deal of damage to your self-esteem, and so do the verbal attacks followed by humiliation and betrayal of trust. A feeling of being worthless takes hold of you like a pair of pliers. You have lost all hope, dreams are now nightmares, and your vision of life is now blurred. You seem to float around disassociated from the world. You begin to not care about what happens next, while numb on the inside, wishing you were invisible and hoping no one notices the bruises.

Self-esteem is essential to making the necessary changes in your life. Your self-esteem determines your value and worth. It also helps to protect you from future problems. In order to live the very best life we have to work on re-building our self-esteem. You must learn to love yourself outside of someone else's opinion, current job, past events, or living environment. A healthy view of yourself attracts positive things and positive people into your life. Walking around with baggage and an on-going pity party attracts more negative things and negative people.

Traits of High Self-esteem

Self-esteem **is your belief or opinion of you.** Have you been programmed to believe you are worthless, undeserving, and helpless in life? Were you programmed to have low self-esteem? Low self-esteem can make you feel like you are always the victim. **With daily practice you can re-build your self-esteem and have more confidence. Here are some tips to boost your self-esteem.**

1. **Believe in Yourself: Don't bother yourself with a lot of negative self-talk. Find ways to improve that area. Find what you** are good at and your own abilities. Low self-esteem can send you pointing the finger at everyone and everything else that you can possibly find to blame for not succeeding. Be accountable for your actions, don't make excuses, or blame others.
2. **Know what YOU want**: Have clear specific ideas about what you want or need. Be able to assert your needs and wants to others.
3. **Desire to succeed:** Learn from your failures and then move on. Being flexible makes it easier to overcome challenges and disappointments along the way. Know your strengths and develop them while focusing on the weaknesses as well.
4. **Goal-orientated: Fo**cus on self-improvement and success. Plan and set goals for yourself. Learn new skills that will move you closer to reaching and achieving your goals. Seek

Self-Esteem

self-awareness and self-approval to achieve your goals.
5. **Self-awareness:** Learn yourself. Look within you and bring yourself out. As you gain knowledge and become more familiar with yourself, you will begin to see yourself differently and so will others.
6. **Self-approval:** Forgive yourself and others that hurt you. Grant yourself permission to move on. Seek new opportunities and take hold of the fulfillment those opportunities bring. Look for the goodness inside of you. Do what YOU like and own your choices. No outside approval needed.

I took practical steps in re-building my self-esteem. One easy step was smiling for no reason. I smiled at people I didn't know. This felt weird at first and later became a game to see how many people would smile back. Some smiled back. Some didn't.

I pulled out all my awards, thank you cards, love letters, recommendation letters, certificates, degrees, and other small tokens that had been given to me over the years. I placed them around my desk at home to remind me of my achievements. This gave me daily confidence and the re-assurance I needed especially when I felt I couldn't do something or when fear would try to creep in.

As I mentioned in Chapter Four, I spoke love to myself by looking in the mirror and telling myself good things, patting myself on the back first, encouraging myself to do more, and pushing myself to new limits. I became my own coach.

He Loves Me Not

We sometimes overlook our self-esteem until we face difficulties or hit rock bottom. What you think about yourself is a major part of building your self-esteem, but also your actions must be positive to receive the reward of fulfillment. It's simply taking time out for you.

Knowing What You Want is Half the Challenge

People usually get what they want because they **know** what they want. For many years, I was lost and without a clue of what I wanted in life or who I wanted to be. To help you get on the right path, I put together a list of basic questions to help figure out what you want. Write your answers on a separate piece of paper so you can reflect back on your answers.

Take a moment to look at some of the areas in your life (family, career, home, finances, health, etc.). Where are you dissatisfied?

Career and Education

1. What experiences have you had that gave you an unusual sense of purpose?
2. Do you want to continue your education?
3. Do you want to get a two year (Associates) or a four year degree (Bachelors)?
4. What do you want to major in?
5. What would people who know you well say about what you are made to do?
6. What would you like to do in your life?
7. What are some of your key learned skills?
8. What skills do you want to master?

Life and Home

1. What in your environment worries you or uses up your energy?
2. What does marriage mean to you? Would you like to be married?
3. Do you want children?
4. What could you change about you that would change your situation?
5. What fears, doubts, or other internal obstacles are keeping you from moving forward with your life?
6. What do you feel is a better choice: to buy a home or rent? What were the deciding factors to make this choice?
7. What monthly payment would you be comfortable making for rent or a mortgage?
8. Where would you like to live?

Finance and Credit

1. What are some 'things' you could buy that you believe would make you happy? Which one will really make the most difference?
2. How much money do you want to save per year?
3. Do you want to invest money in stocks, 401K, IRAs, or CDs?
4. Do you have a checking and savings account?
5. What is your credit score?

Health and Personal Development
1. What about your health? Are you tolerating or coping with any issues?
2. Do you exercise?
3. When was your last annual check-up?
4. Are you the desired weight you want to be?
5. Five years from now where do you want to be?
6. What is something you would like to learn?
7. Imagine yourself at a time in the future when you are living your ideal life. How does it look?
8. Describe your relationship with God. What is it like?
9. What's missing?

Self-Esteem

NOTES

He Loves Me Not

CHAPTER SIX

Victim to Victor

Three days into writing this book I became emotionally overwhelmed recalling my past moments of victimization. It never dawned on me how much adversity and pain I had overcome. The pain and suffering was way too much for anyone to go through. What is written on the pages of this book is only a small portion of my pain. I couldn't help but to think and question myself on how I made it through all this drama.

I don't consider myself as strong, even though I've gone through so much. There were many times when I wanted to stop fighting and just give up. But it was the words of encouragement from family and friends that kept me going.

My Mess, His Grace
I recall a time during my teenage years when I decided I had had enough of life. The hole in my heart sucked my energy, the pain

weighed too much and made it hard for me to smile. I sat on the floor with my back against the couch, head down as I reach for the bottle. I opened a prescription bottle filled with white capsules and looked for the glass of juice I had prepared to wash the pills down with. One by one, I put each pill in my mouth and swallowed until they were all gone.

I called up a close friend to say my goodbyes, crying as I told her about all the pills I had taken. It wasn't long afterwards, there was a knock at the door. It was the paramedics coming to get me. My friend had called an ambulance.

I remember my body going airborne a few times as the ambulance sped to the hospital. I wanted them to slow down to give the pills time to work. I didn't want to live. Shortly, I heard the unlatching of the ambulance doors and they hurried me inside. As I laid there in the hospital bed looking up at the ceiling waiting for the lights to go out and never come back on, my doctor walked up next to my bed. He informed me that the pills I had taken were harmless. I didn't speak. I just laid there still waiting to die. Nothing happened.

I had failed at my own suicide. I was discharged that day and left the hospital feeling even worse about myself afterwards than I had before I had taken the pills. Still here, still stuck.

In 2014, I attended a Leaderpreneur Conference hosted by Delatorro McNeal II in Florida. During a group exercise, Delatorro called out a series of questions and asked for volunteers to step forward inside a circle of 100 attendees if the question was true or applied to you. About thirty minutes in to the session, Delatorro then called for individuals who had attempted to commit suicide to step forward. Without thought or hesitation I looked up and I was in the middle of the circle. It was as if someone else was moving my feet and had placed me in the middle of the circle. I had been called out.

I wasn't sure what to expect at this point and waited in the middle of the circle until Delatorro spoke. My heart pounded rapidly as if I had run five miles to get to the middle of the room. I was so nervous and I started to feel as though I was going to faint right there in the middle of the floor while everyone was watching.

There was pure silence. You could have heard a cotton ball drop. It was so quiet. Delatorro made eye contact, turning his head slowly; pausing long enough to make sure he connected with the few that stood in the group. Then he congratulated us. My left eye brow rose in confusion, unsure of what I just heard. I had quickly prepared myself for a good scolding for the selfish act I had attempted. But a scolding was far from the conversation. Delatorro congratulated us for failing; failing to kill ourselves. Delatorro said, "Had it not been for your failure, you wouldn't be standing here today."

My body weakened and bent over with thanks as the tears flowed. It was a cry of all cries. It came from my gut up to my eyes. I had cried many times before, but this cry was different. It was a cry of gratitude and joy as the tears streamed down my face. Life, that had once been taken for granted, became real and so precious at that very moment.

I thank God for his mercy and his grace for keeping me here. I've never been so happy for failing in all my days. The thought of not being here because of what I thought was so bad at the time it makes my heart sink.

Sadly, as I sat in a meeting, a lady told a story about her neighbor's daughter who had hung herself to death. The little girl was only in the 6th grade. It could have been me. I thought to myself of how blessed I am. I was still here and had the opportunity to get it right. She, on the other hand, had succeeded at suicide and would never get another chance at conquering life.

God used my mess to deliver this message. God is waiting for you to ask for His help.

The Decision

I was told a lie. As a matter of fact there were many of them, lies that never really sat well with me. But they would keep me in bondage and tangled up in my enemy's web of tricks. You can choose to remain a victim or you can choose to use that pain for something greater than you and become a victor. Conquer life.

In my role as a victim I carried the feeling of hopelessness and told myself maybe this was the way things were. I did very little to change my circumstances, always felt powerless and unaccountable for why or what happened in my life. I chose to sit in darkness. I chose to do nothing to change my life.

The transformation started with one decision; THE DECISION to make a decision. Sounds real simple and yes, it is. But there were many times I failed to make that one decision. Instead, I chose to give my control to others and settle for whatever life handed out.

Everything we do is a decision; even not making a decision is a decision. Each decision will either enhance your life or drain your life. Setting goals, managing money, saving, starting a business, purchasing a house, getting married, leaving a toxic relationship, or writing a book all start with making the decision to act.

After the decision is made, finding out what the necessary steps are is next. This is where you have to put in some time and effort. When I made the choice that I would not enter into another abusive relationship, I had to find out exactly what a real relationship was. From there I decided what I wanted my new relationship to look like and added or removed some things from my life so I could have the relationship I wanted.

I set some ground rules for myself and used them to shape the life I wanted to have.

Becoming a victor is not only forgiving the people that wronged you and setting new boundaries, it's about making better decisions, creating a plan, and taking action.

The first step in transforming from a victim to a victor is

acknowledging you have full control of your life. Take your life back. Choose to make better decisions and make the appropriate changes in life. Learn from your experiences. All experiences have a lesson to be learned. The lessons often repeated are likely the ones in which we failed to identify the actions that caused the experience. This means that if you are doing the same thing you are likely to get the same results. If you don't like something in your life, acknowledge you don't like it and change it.

Secondly, keep your focus on you, not your past pain. Focus on your weaknesses and develop your strengths. What are the areas that need your attention (self-esteem, job skills, communication, time management, patience, etc.)? A quitter will never win or accomplish much. And whining and complaining doesn't do any good either. There may be struggles and obstacles along the way, but the reward will always outweigh the pain endured.

Thirdly, know what you want. Decide what you want and how it will benefit your life. Identifying what you want in life creates a map. When you get it you know you have arrived at your destination. This brings happiness.

I called up the credit union and asked for a new auto loan. The loan officer called me back about three days later to let me know I had been approved and I could go pick out the car I wanted. I had done my research and knew what the going price was for the car I was looking to purchase. I had a pretty clear picture of what

I wanted. Right down to the color, miles, make and model of the car. On the first stop, the car I test drove had too many miles. The second stop, I got in the car and proceeded to pull off to take the car for a test drive. The car was the right color, had great mileage and a good price. I was feeling real confident. It wasn't long after pulling off when I heard a funny noise. I asked the car salesman if he heard anything. He denied hearing anything. I continued out of the lot, but in a very slow roll. I was sure something was wrong. So I parked the car, got out, and walked around the car. You wouldn't believe it. The whole tire was coming off the car. The salesman called the service center to find out what was going on with the car. While waiting, he had three of their top salesmen approach me trying to sell me a different car. At this point, I didn't want any car off the lot. I was ready to go. I knew what I wanted, so I didn't settle for anything else. Needless to say, I purchased the car I wanted two days later at a different car lot.

Fourthly, be honest and open about your desires. Choose what is best for you not what you feel someone thinks you should have. Writing this book about child molestation and domestic violence wasn't an easy task. As a matter fact, I often wondered what people would say about me exposing the truths; who would get offended, or how my family would feel. It was that same fear that tempted me to stop and that gave me the fuel to finish this book. People needed to know they were not alone and that abuse is wrong. I have a passion for helping others and if that means being transparent to get my message across, then that's what I'll do.

Fifthly, never lose sight of your dreams. You may have to give up some old habits and ways, even people to reach your goals and live out your dreams. Eliminate distractions, wasted effort, and continue to chase after your dreams.

Finally, love yourself first. I cannot express this enough. People will often view you based on how you view yourself. Love yourself more by not compromising to please others. Love yourself enough to keep trying and striving for more, something for you.

I pray from this point on you seek a positive perspective on life and that you use your pain and failures as opportunities to improve your life. I can say that my past gave me my strength, birthed my courage, and fueled my drive to succeed. I believe life is truly what you make of it. No matter what it looks like right now, you can change it. It's only temporary unless you make it permanent.

Choose something different.

He Loves Me Not

NOTES

Victim to Victor

He Loves Me Not

20 Principles of Loving Yourself More

Be true to yourself. Do not betray yourself by over compromising to please others. At the end of the day you will be unhappy and they'll keep asking for more. Be who you are, compromise but not at the expense of your own self respect, learn to say NO.

Respect yourself. Do not let anyone disrespect you. What you accept from others is what they will give you. You teach people how you want to treated.

Do not give wife benefits to a boyfriend. If you give him everything before marriage, what will he have to look forward to?

God will give you the <u>desires</u> of your heart. The enemy gives you what you want and then you find out you really didn't want that at all.

You have the POWER to change your life. Do not whine or complain long about your issues. Do something about them.

Do not over look what hurts you. If something hurts your mind, spirit, ears, body or your heart get rid of it. Address the issue right then.

Give your time to people that deserve it. Your time is valuable and must be earned. Everyone does not deserve your time.

Learn from your mistakes. Reduce the amount of mistakes

20 Principles of Loving Yourself More

and redo's. Look over it twice even three times if needed before calling it the final.

Do what you love. Do a lot of what makes you HAPPY. Try new things.

Make good decision. Every decision you make will either compliment or drain your life.

Set Boundaries. What is acceptable? What makes you feel good? What is crossing the line? Stand up for yourself.

Do not give to gain friendship. Friendship is free.

Do not do anything that makes you feel bad afterwards. If it makes you feel guilty, sad, upset, or angry, don't do it again.

If it does not benefit you remove it from your life.

Do not try to fix anyone. You are not SUPERWOMAN.

Know the difference between Going through and Growing through. Going through is non rational and you continue to go through the same things over and over. Growing through you will not continue the same path; you will learn what works best and move on to the next level.

Be honest about your past but be careful not to go into too much detail. Let the past be the past.

You are a mirror image of the 5 people you spend the most time with. Watch the company you keep.

You are like a raw coin. Are you trying to be like everyone else? Stop trying to be a quarter when you are a Gold dollar.

Make your own rules.

Victims' Bill of Rights

I have the right to be treated with respect and honor.

I have the right to not be yelled at, demeaned, threatened, intimidated, hit, shoved, have sex, or be touched without my permission.

I have the right to express my opinions and ideas, even if they are different from the opinions and ideas of others.

I have the right to live without humiliation, manipulation, corruption, isolation, neglect, ridicule, or other emotional assault.

I have the right to all information that concerns my welfare, including financial, medical, and legal facts.

I have the right to participate equally in making decisions that affect me.

I have the right to expect you to be honest and to keep your promises and agreements.

Victims' Bill of Rights

I have the right to socialize with friends of my choice.

I have the right to worship as I please.

I have the right to spend time by myself.

I have the right to the support of law enforcement and the judicial system if I am violated.

I have the right to reserve my trust in you until it is earned by your exhibition of integrity, trustworthy and credible behavior.

About the Author

Referred to as "**Strong and Courageous**" Kimesha Coleman wants nothing more than to help clients progress from victim to victor by overcoming insecurities and low self-esteem. The President and CEO of Kimesha Coleman Coaching, Kimesha is a life coach,

About the Author

motivational speaker, and the author of *He Loves Me Not: Buried Tears of Betrayed Love*. Her book inspires readers with its candid format, each chapter a portrayal of her remarkable story, which she adeptly transforms into motivational jewels.

Prior to coaching professionally, Kimesha mentored women in domestic violence and emergency situations. As a survivor of abuse, she had a sincere desire to help others and this aspiration led to advising women at Concord Baptist Church in the Restoring Vessels, a single mother's ministry, Genesis Shelter for battered women and Hope Mansion for women in crisis. Kimesha is a Motivational Speaker, Facilitator, and Sexual & Domestic Violence Advocate and recently had the privilege of speaking for God's Women of Purpose and Unlocking Your Potential Women's Enrichment Seminar in the Dallas area. She has also hosted job readiness training for battered women at Genesis Shelter.

As a Life Strategist and Transformation Coach, she has a passion for helping others bypass the setbacks she has personally experienced, break free from their invisible jail, overcome barriers, and find their purpose by discovering their greatness.

Kimesha understands hardships and knows exactly how it feels to live in fear or in a state of uncertainty, but it is her quest to help others find clarity. Her compassion, expertise and sterling reputation are factors new and existing clients have come to depend on. Kimesha's goal is to bring hope to the hopeless, to empower and transform lives and she wishes to be a stepping stone toward the brighter, more promising future you deserve.

For additional information and products please visit http:www.*coachingbykimesha.com*. To book Kimesha for your next event, please contact kc@coachingbykimesha.com.

References

Chapman, Gary, The Five Love Languages: Singles Edition. (2004)

Greenhaven Press, Inc., Child Sexual Abuse. (1998)

Leakes, Nene, Never Make the Same Mistake Twice. (2009)

Lissette, Andrea and Kraus, Richard, Free Yourself from an Abusive Relationship. (2000)

Kearney, Dr. R. Timothy, Caring for Sexually Abused Children. (2001)

Scott, Lindquist, The Date Rape Prevention Book. (2000)

Smith, Gerrilyn, The Protectors Handbook: Reducing the risk of child abuse and helping children recover. (1997)

Shire, Priscilla, The Resolution for Women. (2011)

Tirabassi, Becky and Roger, Let Love Change Your Life. (1998)

Discover God Study Bible: New Living Translation, Tyndale House Publishing. (2007)

References

National Center for Injury Prevention and Control, Atlanta, Georgia, Costs of Intimate Partner Violence Against Women in the United States, Department of Health and Human Services, Centers for Disease Control and Prevention. (March 2003*)*

www.ingramcontent.com/pod-product-compliance
Lightning Source LLC
Chambersburg PA
CBHW051658040426
42446CB00009B/1197